I'm Saved … What's Next? Study Guide

Building a Relationship 10 Keys to Walk with God

BRENDA R. ROBY

WESTBOW
P R E S S®
A DIVISION OF THOMAS NELSON
& ZONDERVAN

WestBow Press books may be ordered through booksellers or by contacting:

WestBow Press
A Division of Thomas Nelson & Zondervan
1663 Liberty Drive
Bloomington, IN 47403
www.westbowpress.com
844-714-3454

Scripture taken from the Amplified Bible, Copyright © 1954, 1958, 1962, 1964, 1965, 1987 by The Lockman Foundation. Used with permission.

ISBN: 978-1-6642-3972-2 (sc)
ISBN: 978-1-6642-3974-6 (hc)
ISBN: 978-1-6642-3973-9 (e)

Library of Congress Control Number: 2021913844

Print information available on the last page.

WestBow Press rev. date: 07/22/2021

To all new believers. Always study to show yourself approved unto God ... rightly dividing the word of truth. May you be encouraged on this journey to become the *uncommon* (exceptional) you.

Contents

Acknowledgements

I am forever grateful to my cousin, Apostle Orlando Bembry, for hearing from God concerning a workbook to accompany *I'm Saved ... What's Next?* Without you having heard the voice of God, this study guide might not exist. So thanks for being a mighty man of God, and I pray that everything God has planned for you comes to fruition.

A very special thanks to my support team: my husband and family for your endless encouragement. My prayer is that God will continue to shine His face upon you and bless you indeed for continuously standing with me.

Using This Study Guide

The study guide was a divine plan of God. He knew that people needed something that would take them step by step in the beginning phase of their walk with Him. It is being used in connection with the book *I'm Saved ... What's Next?* in order to assist you in handling daily situations God's way. In order for you to shine your light for Jesus, you must be equipped with the basics. Learning how to handle yourself in times like we are experiencing now is of great importance. No matter how difficult it might get, or when there are circumstances you might not understand, do not give up. Greater is He who is in you than he who is in the world.

The study guide is designed to assist you in your study time. Incorporating the book with the Bible aids in bringing clarity to your walk with God in a simplistic way. By reading each chapter in the book *I'm Saved ... What's Next?* coupled with researching scriptures and subsequently answering the related questions in the study guide, this process will help you gain better knowledge of each topic, equipping you to better handle situations when they arise. There is also an answer key at the end of this book to further assist you in properly modeling the behaviors of Christ.

Study with purpose. Gather your resources: book, study guide, Bible, paper, and pencil. Go to a quiet place where you can focus on the materials and hear from God. Begin your study with a time of praise and worship. You always want to invite the Holy Spirit into your session of learning. We encourage you to take control of your challenges every day by doing it God's way! You can do all things through Christ who strengthens you (Philippians 4:13).

Each chapter in this study guide contains the following sections:

- **Key questions**. Reinforces your knowledge of the book as well as scriptural verses. The questions are to pique your curiosity about each key while also assessing your knowledge about the topic. They help you to put information into your own words, which aids in memory of the principles.

- **Exercises**. Helps you to understand the principles and apply each key to your life. The exercises allow you to put God's values into practice by resolving issues His way, therefore building your faith. The exercises are your faith builders, for faith without works is dead (James 2:17).

- **Declarations**. Encourages you to believe what God has said about you. They help to confirm and affirm what you believe (your assurance and confidence in God). They get you in the habit of saying what God says so that as you mix in your faith, these words will have the power they had when God Himself spoke them. These declarations will push you into your breakthrough and set the direction for your life, because life and death are in the power of your tongue (Proverbs 18:21).

- **Scripture references.** Each declaration is used to assist you in speaking the Word only. By adding the scripture underneath, you can review the actual passage for study. These declarations show you how to take a scripture and confess it over your situation. Words are seeds; sow (speak) wisely because you will have whatsoever you say (Mark 11:24).

All sections are geared toward you learning each key so that you can effectively walk it out daily in your life. The book *I'm Saved ... What's Next?* paired with the study guide will jump-start your Christian walk and help build your relationship with God. They were designed to encourage you to live your life every day, God's way! Your new life awaits you.

Introduction

Beginning your new walk with Christ can be a roller coaster. There are many ups and downs and twists and turns, so hold on. Regardless, this life is the best life ever. It may seem difficult, it may seem like you have to give up a lot, but in actuality, the Christian life is easy. It's the way of the transgressor (non-Christian) that is hard (Proverbs 13:15).

You are now in position to turn things around in your life. It will take time and your willingness to work at it, but it can be done. The benefit totally outweighs the cost. I ask you to go on this journey with Christ expecting to see change in your life. Patience and dedication are the keys. Learning how to change your thought patterns will be the most important part of this walk. Your mind is the battleground, and your actions follow your thoughts. You must submit yourself to God's way of doing things and be determined to follow suit no matter what. It's going to be difficult at first because it will go against all that your flesh (the old you) is telling you to do, think, and say. But stay focused, and don't cheat yourself out of experiencing the abundant life here on earth and spending eternity with Christ.

God loves you so much and wants to have a deep and loving relationship with you. The study guide is here to assist you along your path to building your relationship with God. Enjoy this time of growing in Christ.

Key #1

Love

Before you begin, read Key 1 in *I'm Saved ... What's Next?*

1. According to *I'm Saved ... What's Next?*, what are the four types of love? _____

    _____

    _____

    _____

2. Which type of love is the greatest? _____

    Why? _____

3. Read 1 John 4:8, Ephesians 1:4–5, and Luke 6:31.

    a. In building a relationship with God, you must understand

        that God is _____.

    b. He planned to love you and adopt you as His own child

        because _____

        _____.

c. According to *I'm Saved ... What's Next?*, you are to treat people how you would like them to treat you, not _____.

d. Why do you think God wants us to do this? _____

_____

4. Read Matthew 22:35–40.

a. What is the greatest commandment? _____

_____

_____

_____

_____

b. What is the second? _____

_____

_____

_____

_____

5. Read 1 John 4:20, Matthew 18:21–22, and Ephesians 4:32.

a. Can you love God and hate your brother? _____

_____

_____

Why or why not? _____

_____

_____

b. _____

is a major part of the love walk with Christ.

c. How many times must we forgive others? _____

d. What do you think was the message that Jesus was really trying to say concerning forgiveness? _____

_____

_____

6. Read 1 Corinthians 13:5 and Leviticus 19:18.

a. Have you ever told someone, "I forgive you, but I won't forget"? _____

_____

b. Was there a time that you reminded someone of a past error? _____

_____

c. If you have, knowing what you now know about God's love, were you acting in love? _____

_____

d. How would you handle the situation today? _____

_____

_____

_____

_____

_____

Exercise

Gauge your love walk by reading 1 Corinthians 13:4–8a. In every place where love is mentioned or referenced, ask yourself, "Am I patient? Am I kind? Am I envious?" This exercise will help you see where you are on your love walk with Christ. Be truthful and be willing to do the work that is necessary to begin walking in God's perfect love. Take each section and ask Jesus to reveal to you how to walk in love daily, and He will because He loves you so much and wants you to be who God created you to be.

Please note: this exercise will not be completed in one day, week, or month. This will be an ongoing, continual process. As Christians, we should always be evaluating our love walk, making sure we're looking and acting like our big brother, Jesus.

Declaration

God is love. He loves me more than I'll ever know. With the love, compassion, forgiveness, and patience that He showers upon me constantly, I will share this same unconditional love with others. I am a product of God's love, and I will use it to bring glory to His name. In Jesus's name, amen.

Scripture References

1 John 4:8, 16

Key #2

Trust

Before you begin, read Key 2 in *I'm Saved ... What's Next?*

Read Proverbs 3:5-6. Fill in the blanks:

1. _____ in the Lord with

   _____ and lean not unto your own

   _____; in

   _____ acknowledge Him, and He shall direct your paths.

2. God said He will direct your path. What does that mean?

   _____

   _____

3. According to *I'm Saved ... What's Next?*, what is the meaning
   of the acronym TRUST? _____

   _____

   _____

4. Read Jeremiah 29:11.

    Why do you think God wants us to wait on His timing?

    _____

    _____

    _____

5. Read John 16:33 and 1 Peter 1:7 (ERV).

    a. Even though we will experience trials and tribulations in this world and sometimes it may seem like they never end, what does Jesus say we have in Him? _____

    b. What is actually on trial when you are being tested?

        _____

    c. Why is your faith more precious than gold? _____

        _____

        _____

        _____

        _____

        _____

6. Read Ephesians 4:22–24 and Romans 12:2.

    a. What is the "old man"? _____

    b. As Christians (new creatures), we must relinquish the ways of the "old man." Why? _____

        _____

        _____

c. God wants you to _____

so that you may prove the good, acceptable, and perfect

will of God.

d. What does it mean to renew your mind? _____

_____

e. When your mind is renewed, then your life will be

transformed. Explain. _____

_____

_____

_____

7. Read James 1:6–7 (EXB) and Hebrews 11:1.

a. What is the dictionary definition of doubt? _____

_____

b. When asking God for anything, how does God want us

to approach Him? _____

_____

c. What does the Bible call those who doubt? _____

_____

d. Why will doubters not receive from the Lord? _____

_____

_____

_____

_____

8. Read Mark 11:23–24, John 15:7, Hebrews 11:3, and Revelation 12:11.

   a. According to *I'm Saved … What's Next?*, trusting God means to say _____.

   b. When God spoke, "Let there be light," what happened?

      _____

   c. When we speak what our situation looks like, what do we get? _____

   d. According to your reading, the enemy wants you to _____.

   e. Why do you think the enemy wants you to say what you see instead of what God says? _____

      _____

      _____

      _____

      _____

      _____

Exercise

Research each scripture and personalize it for your declaration. This is your position when life throws you a curveball. You can write them on index cards to keep handy, and remember to speak the Word only!

- When you are experiencing challenges in your body, you say Isaiah 53:5. Example: "By Jesus's stripes, I am healed."

  _____

  _____

  _____

  _____

  _____

- When you feel alone, you say Deuteronomy 31:6.

  _____

  _____

  _____

  _____

- When you feel overwhelmed, you say Matthew 11:28.

  _____

  _____

  _____

  _____

- When you feel like giving up, you say 1 Peter 5:6–7.

  _____

  _____

  _____

  _____

- When you feel your prayers are not being answered, you say 1 John 5:14.

  _____

  _____

  _____

  _____

- When you feel defeated, you say Psalms 34:19.

  _____

  _____

  _____

  _____

- When you feel restless, you say Romans 8:38–39.

  _____

  _____

  _____

  _____

- When you experience lack in finances, you say Philippians 4:19.

  _____

  _____

  _____

  _____

- When your children are being defiant, you say Colossians 3:20.

_____

_____

_____

_____

Declaration

I am trusting in the Lord with all of my heart. I will not try to figure everything out on my own. In all of my decisions, I will ask the Lord, and He will keep me on the right track. With every step I take, I will listen for His voice, and He will help me go the right way. In Jesus's name, amen.

Scripture Reference

Proverbs 3:5-6

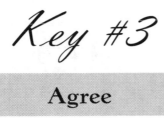

Key #3

Agree

Before you begin, read Key 3 in *I'm Saved ... What's Next?*

1. Read Amos 3:3.

    a. Can two walk together if they are not in agreement?

    _____

    Give an example of this type of situation:

    _____

    _____

    _____

    _____

    _____

    b. According to *I'm Saved ... What's Next?*, when are we in

    agreement with God, _____

    _____

    _____

    _____.

c. What does it mean to walk with God?

_____

_____

_____

_____

_____

2. Read Genesis 6:9, Genesis 17:1, and Luke 1:5–6.

We see several men in the Bible walking with God. What are some of the characteristics we, too, must display in order to walk with God? _____

_____

_____

_____

_____

_____

3. As believers, our walks must match our talk. Explain.

_____

_____

_____

_____

_____

_____

4. Matthew 5:16 (AMP) says, "Let your light shine before men in such a way that they may see your good deeds *and* moral excellence, and [recognize and honor and] glorify your Father who is in heaven" (italics added).

   Explain in your own words.

   _____

   _____

   _____

   _____

   _____

5. Read Romans 12:19.

   a. Should we try to get even with a person who wronged us?

      _____

   b. What should we do? _____

      _____

      _____

      _____

   c. According to *I'm Saved ... What's Next?*, why should we handle it this way? _____

      _____

      _____

      _____

      _____

Exercise

Being in agreement with God means you believe what He says about who you are, what you can do, and what you can have. Your assignment is to begin paying attention to your situations and how you respond to them. Notice if you are saying what God says or if you are saying what you see going on around you. At the end of this book, there is a journaling section for you to write your situation and response. Next, ask yourself if this is God's view or yours. If it is God's, keep up the good work. If not, replace your thought or statement with God's Word concerning it, and keep saying it so that you can have what God says.

Declaration

I choose to speak what God's Word says and not what I see. I speak faith-filled words that will put the spirit of life into operation in my life. I am who God says I am, I have what God says I have, and I can do what God says I can do. I talk like God because I am in total agreement with His Word. In Jesus's name, amen.

Scripture References

Matthew 8:8

Philippians 4:13

Amos 3:3

Key #4

Devote

Before you begin, read Key 4 in *I'm Saved ... What's Next?*

1. Define *devote* in your own words.

   _____

   _____

   _____

   _____

   _____

2. Psalm 37:5 says, "Commit your way to the Lord; trust also in him; and he shall bring it to pass."

   a. What does this scripture mean to you?

   _____

   _____

   _____

   _____

b. Give an example of a situation where you had to apply this scripture.

_____

_____

_____

_____

c. In the above scripture, what is the meaning of "he shall bring it to pass?"

_____

_____

_____

_____

d. Read James 1:3–4.

   What does waiting on the Lord cause you to develop?

_____

_____

e. Why is developing it so important to the believer?

_____

_____

_____

_____

_____

3. Read Romans 12:1–3.

    a. How are we to present our bodies before God?

    _____

    _____

    b. Give an example of a way to present your body as pleasing before God.

    _____

    _____

    _____

    _____

    c. The Bible says this is our reasonable service. Explain what "reasonable service" means to you.

    _____

    _____

    _____

    _____

4. Read Colossians 3:23–24 (KJV).

    a. Whatsoever you do, do it heartily, _____

    and _____

    b. Does this mean that you are not supposed to work and accomplish the tasks your supervisor has given you?

    _____

    _____

c. God is the one who is ultimately judging all we do, and to work heartily means that we work from our soul. We are to do things with passion and with a good attitude to improve our personal lives while influencing others. Give an example (work, home, school) of you working heartily unto the Lord.

_____

_____

_____

_____

5. According to *I'm Saved ... What's Next?*, there are three ways to handle a situation.

   a. What are they?

   _____

   _____

   _____

   _____

   b. Why is it best to choose God's way in handling situations?

   _____

   _____

   _____

   _____

   _____

c. According to *I'm Saved ... What's Next?*, true devotion will

_____

_____

d. According to the book, devotion only works _____

_____

_____

_____

_____

e. Explain the statement above in your own words.

_____

_____

_____

_____

_____

Exercise

No one stumbles into godliness. It takes a disciplined lifestyle to build your relationship with God. Habits shape, inform, and expose where our hearts are. Our lives revolve around what we love. Loving God means our lives should reflect us spending time in His Word to get to know Him personally and then doing what we've learned.

Each day, sacrifice your eyes to look on nothing that's evil; your ears and mouth to hear and say nothing to tear someone down;

and your hands to do no unruly deeds. Allow your eyes, ears, mouth, and hands to do and say those things that will glorify God. This is how you become a living sacrifice that's holy and pleasing unto the Father.

Declaration

I have been bought with a price. God owns my whole works—spirit, body, and soul; therefore, I will love the Lord with all my heart, with all my soul, and with all my might. I glorify the Lord on earth by accomplishing the work that He has given me to do. In every area of my life, I show forth my devotion to God by doing things that will please Him and bring glory to His name. In Jesus's name, amen.

Scripture References

1 Corinthians 6:20

Matthew 22:37

John 8:29

Key #5

Submit

Before you begin, read Key 5 in *I'm Saved ... What's Next?*

1. Define *submit*.

_____

_____

_____

_____

In our culture, no one wants to submit. We do what we want when we want. Submission is an outward demonstration of our obedience to God's way, and it helps us to build our relationship with Him.

2. Read Luke 9:23.

_____

_____

_____

a. What two things must you do to be a follower of Jesus?

_____

_____

_____

b. What does "deny yourself" mean to you?

_____

_____

_____

_____

_____

c. "Take up your cross" means to put Jesus at the center of all your decisions. You deliberately surrender your life and mind by obeying Christ. How often should you do this?

_____

_____

3. Read Romans 13:1-7, Hebrews 13:17, Colossians 3:18, and Ephesians 5:21.

a. List four areas in which we show our submission to God:

_____

_____

_____

_____

4. Some people view submission as a state of weakness. In *I'm Saved ... What's Next?*, submission to God shows your confidence in Him. It causes you to be selfless rather than selfish, and that's _____.

5. Read Luke 22:39–42, Ephesians 1:20–23, Philippians 2:8, and 1 Peter 5:6.

   a. What did Jesus mean when He said, "Not my will, but thine will be done?"

   _____

   _____

   _____

   _____

   b. Where is Jesus seated now?

   _____

   _____

   _____

   _____

   c. Why did God place Jesus in a place of such power?

   _____

   _____

   _____

   _____

d. What will God do when we truly submit ourselves to Him?

_____

_____

_____

_____

6. Read James 4:7 and Mark 1:21–27.

a. Why is it so important to always submit to God?

_____

_____

_____

_____

b. Jesus walked under the authority (submission) of God; therefore, He was also able to use this authority. In what ways can you use this authority?

_____

_____

_____

_____

Exercise

Practice humbly submitting yourself to someone (parent, spouse, teacher, supervisor, church leader, government official, police officer, etc.). Hold your tongue and listen to their plans and ideas. Be willing to follow their instructions without voicing your opinion or complaining. Remember, as you submit to those around you, you are showing submission to God. If you resist authority (not obeying promptly or grumbling), you are opposing what God has put in place, and He will hold you responsible (Romans 13:1–3).

Declaration

I submit myself first to God and then to others because He knows the plans He has for me. They will cause me to prosper. Even though I may experience temporary discomfort, it's OK because God works everything together for my good. He won't hurt me. He has a plan to give me hope and a good future. My future is bright because I trust Him. In Jesus's name, amen.

Scripture References

James 4:7

Galatians 5:21

Jeremiah 29:11

Romans 8:28

Proverbs 3:5–6

Key #6

Humble

Before you begin, read Key 6 in *I'm Saved ... What's Next?*

1. Define *humility*.

   _____

   _____

   _____

   _____

Humility and submission go hand in hand. Humility is an attitude of the heart. Submission is the action that shows what's in your heart. Walking in humility is walking in the likeness of Christ.

2. Humility is having a low self-importance; it's not having a low opinion of yourself.

   a.   What does this mean to you?

   _____

   _____

b. What are some ways you can implement this into your daily activities?

_____

_____

_____

_____

3. Read Proverbs 8:13, 11:2.

a. Humility is a fruit of the Spirit, and it enables you to have a teachable spirit. How would you describe someone with a teachable spirit?

_____

_____

_____

_____

b. Give an example of someone you know who is teachable. What about you? Are you a teachable person? Name a few of your teachable qualities.

_____

_____

_____

_____

_____

c. What blocks humility from working and being seen in your life?

_____

_____

4. Read Psalm 10:4, Romans 12:16, and Proverbs 16:18. What happens to your relationship with God and others when you are prideful?

_____

_____

_____

_____

_____

5. Read James 4:10, Galatians 6:9, Proverbs 11:2, and Philippians 2:5–11.

a. What happens when we humble ourselves before God?

_____

_____

_____

_____

b. Jesus was a servant. A servant is someone who is humble, submits themselves to God, and builds up and encourages those being served. In what ways did Jesus serve humanity doing His time on earth? Read Luke 4:18.

_____

_____

_____

_____

c. List a few ways you demonstrate servanthood in your daily walk.

_____

_____

_____

_____

Exercise

Research *humble* and list five ways you could demonstrate humility in your daily Christian walk.

1. _____

_____

_____

2. _____

_____

_____

3. _____

_____

_____

4. _____

_____

_____

5. _____

_____

_____

Declaration

I am thankful that humility and submission go hand in hand. The Word says that whoever humbles themselves as a child is the greatest in the kingdom. Therefore, I commit myself to God with a childlike heart. I am ready to learn and to serve others as God fills me with His love. Jesus was a servant, and I'm here to imitate Him and bring honor and glory to God's name. I look not only to my interests but also to the interests of others. I prefer others over myself and give them the benefit. Every day, I shine my light brightly before others that they may see my good works and glorify my Father in heaven. In Jesus's name, amen.

Scripture References

Matthew 18:4

Matthew 20:28

1 Corinthians 11:1

Romans 12:10

Matthew 5:16

Ask Every Day

Before you begin, read Key 7 in *I'm Saved ... What's Next?*

Asking (praying to God) every day shows your dependence on Him. You need God to intervene in your situations daily, so go before Him earnestly with the right heart, attitude, and motive. Here is a way to receive from God:

Write each scripture in the space below.

1. a. Mark 11:24

    _____

    _____

    _____

    _____

    _____

    _____

b. John 15:7

_____

_____

_____

_____

c. James 4:3

_____

_____

_____

_____

d. 1 John 5:14–15

_____

_____

_____

_____

e. Review the above scriptures. Will you always get whatever
    you ask for in prayer?

_____

_____

_____

_____

_____

f. Why or why not?

_____

_____

_____

_____

g. How do you receive answered prayers from the Lord?

_____

_____

_____

_____

2. In *I'm Saved ... What's Next?*, what does God look at when we pray? Why?

_____

_____

_____

_____

3. After you pray, according to the book, what must you do?

_____

_____

_____

_____

_____

4. What must always be the believer's stance?

_____

_____

_____

_____

_____

5. According to the book, the Christian's mantra is "I believe; therefore, I see." What does that mean to you?

_____

_____

_____

_____

_____

You have begun building your relationship with God—trusting His plan, agreeing with His Word, and humbling yourself before Him. Now your heart is positioned to properly ask every day for your desires. Before praying to God, your heart has to be positioned and conditioned for the journey. Some prayers are answered instantaneously, some take time to manifest, and many may not come the way you expected, but having a heart that's conditioned for the journey enables you to get through the times of seeming delay.

Exercise

Here's how you build your repertoire of scripture so you can stand. Research the scriptures and write them in the blank spaces.

Part 1: Ask and be specific.

Before asking, check your heart and the Word of God to make sure what you are about to ask for lines up with His will; otherwise, you will not receive. James 4:3 says, "You ask and do not receive, because you ask amiss, that you may spend *it* on your pleasures."

    a. Matthew 7:7

_____

_____

_____

_____

    b. John 15:7

_____

_____

_____

    c. James 1:5–8

_____

_____

_____

d. In *I'm Saved ... What's Next?*, it says that we cannot be double-minded and expect to receive from God. What is the meaning of *double-minded*?

_____

_____

_____

e. Give an example of a situation where a person is being double-minded.

_____

_____

_____

Part 2: Believe.

a. Matthew 21:22

_____

_____

_____

b. Hebrews 11:6

_____

_____

_____

c. 2 Corinthians 5:7

_____

_____

_____

Part 3: Wait.

In your waiting is where the battle for your answer lies. You must be patient and continue to praise and trust God. These will assist you in remaining focused and confident in God until your promise manifests.

a. Lamentations 3:25 (Patient)

_____

_____

_____

b. Romans 12:12 (Patient)

_____

_____

_____

c. Psalms 106:1 (Praise)

_____

_____

_____

d. Proverbs 3:5 (Trust)

_____

_____

_____

Declaration

I bring my petitions before God daily and invite Him to work in my life as He sees fit. God's will be done. I thank God in advance for answered prayers. I believe that I receive my petitions when I pray. I declare that I am standing strong and waiting patiently for my answers. I desire what God wants for me. He guides me in ways to help Him with what is on His heart. He has a longing for souls. Therefore, I ask for an outpouring of God's love, joy, peace, wisdom, and compassion so that I may assist whoever the Lord sees fit this day. My steps are ordered by the Lord, and I do great exploits because He hears and answers my prayers. In Jesus's name, amen.

Scripture References

Philippians 4:6	Psalm 23:3
Matthew 6:10	2 Peter 3:9
Mark 11:24	Psalm 37:23
Ephesians 6:10	Daniel 11:32
Psalm 27:14	1 John 5:15

Key #8

Meditation and Application

Before you begin, read Key 8 in *I'm Saved ... What's Next?*

1. Read Joshua 1:8.

   a. What does it mean to *meditate?*

     _____

     _____

     _____

     _____

     _____

   b. Why do you think God wants you to meditate on His Word day and night?

     _____

     _____

     _____

     _____

2. a. In *I'm Saved … What's Next?*, it mentions that what you think about is very important on your journey with Christ. Complete this sentence: _____

_____ are unspoken words, and

_____

_____; therefore, you must sow wisely.

b. What does "sow wisely" mean to you?

_____

_____

_____

_____

c. Why is it important to watch your words?

_____

_____

_____

_____

3. a. There's a warning given in our reading: "Satan knows the scriptures," but what is his goal?

_____

_____

_____

_____

b. Who did Satan try to trap with this tactic?

_____

_____

_____

_____

c. Read Matthew 4:1–11. How must we defeat Satan's attempts?

_____

_____

_____

_____

4. Read Luke 6:45.

a. If your heart is filled with the Word of God, what comes out of it?

_____

_____

b. Fill your heart with the Word of God because you will be tested (life's challenges). What is the meaning of "out of the abundance of your heart the mouth speaks"?

_____

_____

_____

c. Can this be an indication of your faith level? Why?

_____

_____

_____

_____

d. If you notice that your responses are more like how you used to act, what must you do?

_____

_____

_____

_____

As you have meditated, focused on, and allowed God's truths to make an impact on your heart and spirit, you're now ready to begin applying God's Word to your life. Read James 1:22 and Luke 6:46–49.

5. a. Why is it important to not only hear but also do what God says?

_____

_____

_____

_____

_____

b. What happens when you don't apply God's Word to your life?

_____

_____

_____

_____

c. According to *I'm Saved ... What's Next?*, what are four things you must do when applying God's Word to your life?

_____

_____

_____

_____

d. According to our reading, what depends on you obeying God?

_____

_____

_____

_____

6. Read Ephesians 4:32–5:2 and 1 Corinthians 11:1.

a. What does it mean to imitate?

_____

_____

_____

_____

b. As Christians, how are we to model our lives after Christ?

_____

_____

_____

_____

7. Read Colossians 3:23–4:1.

a. What does the phrase "do it heartily as to the Lord and not to men" mean to you?

_____

_____

_____

_____

b. Give an example of how you completed a task to honor the Lord.

_____

_____

_____

_____

Exercise

Set aside fifteen to thirty minutes a day. Find a quiet spot that's away from distractions. Take a scripture and go before God with an attitude of thanksgiving. Read and reread your chosen passage of scripture and quiet your heart and mind. Take notes, memorize passages, and seek similar scriptures that will aid in your understanding so you can accurately apply it to your life.

Declaration

I will meditate on the Word of God day and night so that I will have great success. I understand the importance of obeying the Word of God. I declare that I am a hearer and a doer of the Word. My desire is to work passionately as to the Lord in everything I do, whether at home, work, church, or school. I choose to do what the Word says to do, act how it instructs me to act, say what it informs me to say, and live the way it tells me to live. I am protected because I am the wise one who built their house on the rock. In Jesus's name, amen.

Scripture References

Joshua 1:8

James 1:22

Colossians 3:23

Matthew 7:24

Key #9

Walk by the Spirit

Before you begin, read Key 9 in *I'm Saved ... What's Next?*

1. According to *I'm Saved ... What's Next?*, we are a three-part being. What is our makeup?

   _____

   _____

   _____

   _____

   _____

2. What is the spirit of the world trying to get you to do?

   _____

   _____

   _____

   _____

   _____

3. According to the book, "it's time to take control of your life."

    a. What are the four ways to accomplish this?

    _____

    _____

    _____

    _____

    b. How can each aspect prove beneficial to your life?

    _____

    _____

    _____

    _____

4. Read Galatians 5:19–25.

    a. List at least five characteristics of the flesh:

    _____

    _____

    _____

    _____

    b. List the nine characteristics of the fruit of the Spirit:

    _____

    _____

    _____

    _____

c. "Walk by the Spirit and ye shall not fulfill the lust of the flesh" (Galatians 5:16). Why?

_____

_____

_____

_____

_____

d. According to our reading, when you walk by the Spirit, you always win. Why?

_____

_____

_____

_____

_____

Exercise

Apply it to your life. Walking in the Spirit has several benefits:

- Walking in goodness (uprightness, integrity, honesty) demonstrates to others we're different from the world.
- Walking in kindness demonstrates to others the love and compassion we have for one another.
- Walking in faithfulness demonstrates our allegiance to Christ and helps to build our relationship with Him.

Fruit of the Spirit: List a way you can demonstrate (show) each fruit in your life:

Love:

_____

_____

_____

_____

Joy:

_____

_____

_____

_____

Peace:

_____

_____

_____

_____

Patience:

_____

_____

_____

Goodness:

_____

_____

_____

_____

_____

Kindness:

_____

_____

_____

_____

_____

Faithfulness:

_____

_____

_____

_____

Gentleness:

_____

_____

_____

_____

Self-Control:

_____

_____

_____

_____

Begin to incorporate them into your daily routines with the help of the Holy Spirit. Allow your actions to flow from a heart of thanksgiving. After a while, it'll become so natural to you, and you'll begin to see a new you.

Declaration

I declare that as I walk by the Spirit, I will not fulfill the desires of my flesh because I keep my mind on Jesus. I allow the fruit of the Spirit to flourish in my life, and as I do so, I walk in humility, I have joy, and I am able to shine God's goodness in this world. In Jesus's name, amen.

Scripture References

Galatians 5:16

Galatians 5:22–23

Matthew 5:16

Key #10

Be Persistent

Before you begin, read Key 10 in *I'm Saved ... What's Next?*

1. Define *persistent*.

_____

_____

_____

_____

_____

_____

2. Give an example of your persistency.

_____

_____

_____

_____

_____

3. According to our reading, why must we be persistent in our faith?

_____

_____

_____

_____

_____

4. You will make mistakes along the way, and you may not see change at first, but do not be dismayed. Why must we keep working God's Word?

_____

_____

_____

_____

_____

5. Research the internet and list five traits of godly character.

_____

_____

_____

_____

_____

_____

6. Every day there is a battle going on, good versus evil. It is important for us to stay focused and choose to do what is good. Can a Christian be influenced by the devil? If so, what are some characteristics believers display that are *not* godly?

_____

_____

_____

_____

_____

7. Read James 4:7. James gives you two things to do in order for the enemy to flee: submit and resist. Explain how to do each in your own words.

   a. Submit to God.

   _____

   _____

   _____

   _____

   b. Resist the devil.

   _____

   _____

   _____

   _____

   _____

8. According to our reading, your weapons are not carnal (fleshy) but are ... _____

_____

_____

_____

_____

_____

Exercise

Review the five traits of godly character that you listed above (question 5). Choose a character trait that you would like/need to develop.

Here's how to begin developing your godly character:

- Be in love with Christ.
- Meditate on His Word concerning this area.
- Be persistent and consistent in applying it to your life (practice this character while engaging with others).

Declaration

Faith without works is dead; therefore, I put feet to my faith by walking in love, forgiveness, and honesty. I will not lose heart or my composure when situations around me go awry, for greater is He who is in me than he who is in the world. I have world-overcoming faith residing in me. I am resilient, I am relentless, and I am a winner because I am persistent in living my life God's way. In Jesus's name, amen.

Scripture References

James 2:17

1 John 4:4

1 John 5:4

Just Doing Church

Key Points

We never stop being the church. Church is more than the building where we worship, more than the two hours on Sunday and Bible study midweek. Being the church is twenty-four seven. It's from the time we wake up until the time we go to bed. It's interacting with those in the body of Christ and those outside. It's being kind to those outside our home and those inside. Being the church is never-ending. As we have received Jesus Christ as our Savior and Lord, we must shine for Jesus every day and in every way.

We must carry ourselves in ways that will bring glory to God. We must walk in love, joy, and peace. We must do the following:

- Move from viewing the church as a location to seeing it as being wherever we are and, most importantly, who we are.
- Move from rituals to relationship.
- Be willing to make a difference.

- Be willing to do missions and outreach work to reach the people.

- Be passionate about the truths of God's Word and walk it out through demonstration.

- Don't go to church just to go, but rather go in order to learn how to be the church.

- Live a lifestyle that's pleasing before God so that He will use it to draw others to Himself.

Walking into Victory

Believe that the God you just committed your life to is the following:

- the one, true, and living God
- omnipotent (all-powerful), omniscient (all-knowing), and omnipresent (ever present)
- righteous, holy, good, true, eternal, self-existent, love, a provider, and your healer

Know who you are in Christ:

- I am a new creation in Christ (2 Corinthians 5:17).
- I am chosen by God, who called me out of darkness into His marvelous light (1 Peter 2:9).
- I can do all things through Christ who strengthens me (Philippians 4:13).
- I have been set free in Christ from the law of sin and death (Romans 8:2).

- I am a child of God and a joint heir with Jesus (Romans 8:16–17).
- I am more than a conqueror through Him who loves me (Romans 8:37).

Believe the Word:

- "Trust in the LORD with all your heart, and lean not on your own understanding; in all your ways acknowledge Him, and He shall direct your paths" (Proverbs 3:5–6).
- "Jesus said to him, if you can believe, all things are possible to him who believes" (Mark 11:23).
- "For we walk by faith, not by sight" (2 Corinthians 5:7).
- "And whatever things you ask in prayer, believing, you will receive" (Matthew 21:22).
- "For with God nothing will be impossible" (Luke 1:37).

Don't live in defeat:

- When life throws you a curveball, keep moving in faith.
- Keep praying.
- Keep declaring God's Word over your situation.
- Keep doing your daily devotionals.
- Keep serving others.

If you stop making forward progress, then you are living in defeat. Jesus didn't die for you to live in defeat. He died so you can have an abundant, joyful, peaceful, loving, and fulfilled life. As you are walking in this, it brings glory to God, and your life shines forth His glory. It also attracts others to you to inquire about this good life.

You must continue to follow after the precepts written in this book and be persistent in your study of God's Word so that you can continue to grow. God is looking for you to increase in your knowledge of Him so that He can increase you.

- "Draw nigh to God, and he will draw nigh to you" (James 4:8).
- "If you abide in Me, and My words abide in you, you will ask what you desire, and it shall be done for you" (John 15:7).
- "May the LORD give you increase more and more, You and your children" (Psalm 115: 14).

You are on an assignment for the Lord. So each day before heading out, put on the whole armor of God (Ephesians 6:11–18). Paul says in Romans 13:14, "But put on the Lord Jesus Christ," so when you put on Jesus's righteousness (choosing to handle situations His way, not in the flesh), essentially, you are clothing yourself with the whole armor of God. You will be walking in peace, your mind will be on things above, not on earthly things, and you'll have the Word ready on your lips to wield it at any time. You can handle whatever may come simply by trusting in God. Situations will arise, but greater is He who is in you than he who is in the world. You are a world overcomer, you are more than a conqueror, and you can do all things through Christ who strengthens you.

I declare that if you take these ten principles of building your relationship with God and mix them with your faith, you'll have that mountain-moving faith that is spoken of in Mark 11:23; you'll be strong in the Lord and in the power of His might. Daily you'll walk in unity alongside God in faith. You'll build your relationship with God and strengthen your love walk with those around you.

Relationship-Building Tools

For additional study, write these scriptures onto index cards to keep handy. Read them daily to have them ready in your arsenal. So when situations occur, this Word will arise in you, and you'll be able to withstand the attack of the enemy. Remember, the Lord Jesus is with you always. He goes with you to fight against your enemies to give you the victory!

- "Be strong and of good courage, do not fear nor be afraid of them; for the LORD your God, He *is* the One who goes with you. He will not leave you nor forsake you" (Deuteronomy 31:6).

- "Trust in the LORD with all your heart, and lean not on your own understanding; in all your ways acknowledge Him, and He shall direct your paths" (Proverbs 3:5–6).

- "For I know the thoughts that I think toward you, says the LORD, thoughts of peace and not of evil, to give you a future and a hope" (Jeremiah 29:11).

- "I am the vine, you are the branches. He who abides in Me, and I in him, bears much fruit; for without Me you can do nothing" (John 15:5).

- "Casting all your care upon Him, for He cares for you" (1 Peter 5:7).

Prayer of Salvation

After reading the book *I'm Saved ... What's Next?* and working through its study guide, if you are excited and encouraged about building your relationship with God but have not received Jesus Christ as your Lord and Savior, now is the perfect time. Romans 10:9 says, "that if you confess with your mouth and believe in your heart that God has raised Him from the dead, you will be saved." Just repeat this prayer aloud:

"Heavenly Father, please forgive me of my sins. I believe that Jesus died for me and You raised Him from the dead. I now submit myself to Lord Jesus to rule and reign in my heart so Your perfect will be accomplished in my life. Fill me, Holy Spirit, with Your presence because You are my Helper, assisting me on this journey. In Jesus's name, I pray. Amen!"

You are now a part of the family of God! Keep reading, studying, and walking out the principles in this book. They will encourage you to stay on the right path. Find yourself a good Bible-based church where you can continue growing in the things of God. Be encouraged and live the good life that Jesus paid the price for you to live!

Journaling Section

_____

_____

_____

_____

_____

_____

_____

_____

_____

_____

_____

_____

_____

_____

_____

_____

_____

Answer Key

Key 1—Love

1. Agape, eros, philia, storge.

2. Agape; the way God loves. It is self-sufficient, it is unconditional.

3. a. Love.

   b. It was His pleasure and His will.

   c. How they are treating you.

   d. You are demonstrating God's kind of love, which enables you to refrain from the need to get revenge.

4. a. Love the Lord your God with all your heart, all your soul, and all your mind.

   b. You shall love your neighbor as yourself (that is, unselfishly; seek the best or higher good for others).

5. a. No; God says that person is a liar. No one can hate their brother that they see every day and say they love God, whom they have never seen.

   b. Forgiveness.

   c. Seventy times seven or seventy-seven times.

d. You must continue to forgive—walk in unlimited forgiveness.

6. a. (Your answer.)

   b. (Your answer.)

   c. No.

   d. (Your answer.)

Key 2—Trust

1. Trust; all your heart; understanding; all your ways.

2. When we rely on God for help or protection and we involve Him in every aspect of our daily lives, then He will go before us and remove some of the obstacles that block our pathways and lead us safely where He has planned.

3. Truly Rely Upon our Savior's Timing.

4. He has a plan for our lives, to do us good and not evil, to give us a future and a hope (an expected end).

5. a. Peace.

   b. Your faith.

   c. When your faith remains strong, it will bring much praise, honor, and glory—your faith will prove God's victory.

6. a. Your former conduct; the way you used to act and think.

   b. Those ways are continuously being corrupted by deceitful lusts, evil thoughts of the heart, and they are contradictory to God's ways, which are holy and righteous (it will interfere with you building a relationship with God).

c. Renew your mind.

d. To be made new in your heart (the spirit/attitude of your mind), to change from handling situations according to the world's system and now begin doing it God's way, using His principles.

e. As you begin to seek the Word of God concerning your situation, you'll begin to see the way you think, feel, and respond begin to change for the better. You'll see God's Word come alive in your life, and people around you will notice a change in you (attitude, character).

7. a. To lack confidence in; distrust; to consider unlikely.

b. In faith (believe).

c. A wave of the sea; blown up and down (driven and tossed) by the wind.

d. When your faith rises and falls, it affects your words and your actions. There is an unsteadiness in your faith, and without faith, it's impossible to please God.

8. a. To say only what the Word says; speak the Word only.

b. Light came into existence.

c. Whatsoever we say (our situation remains the same or gets worse).

d. Speak contrary to God's Word.

e. He wants to ensnare you with your words, causing you to remain in your situations so you will miss out on the blessings God has for you.

Key 3—Agree

1. a. No. (Your response.)

   b. We have the same views and perspective as He does.

   c. To walk with God is to please Him; choosing to obey and live your life by responding His way; you're resembling Jesus on earth.

2. Righteous, integrity, faithful, blameless, honorable, trustworthy, humble, forgiving, loving, and obeying are just a few characteristics.

3. We must be doers of the Word. Our actions must match what we are saying; otherwise, we look unsure in our faith to those around us. We want to be able to convince someone that Jesus is the best way.

4. Live your life in a way that is pleasing before God (walking in love, forgiveness, compassion, peace, etc.). People will see your good deeds and devotion to God and give praise to God because of it.

5. a. No.

   b. We should let God handle it because He'll make sure that true justice will be done.

c. We are obeying God, and because of it, we will inherit a blessing according to 1 Peter 3:9.

Key 4—Devote

1. Devotion to God means you willingly give your time and effort to do things that please God.

2. a. Confidently entrust all (every situation, desire, necessity) to the Lord in prayer and believe for His will to be done, and He will do what is appropriate/necessary for you.
   b. (Your answer.)
   c. God will fulfill/perform His Word (promise).
   d. Patience.
   e. Through trials, your faith gets stronger, and you become mature in your faith, so as trials come along, you won't be easily provoked to quit, but you'll stay in the fight until you win, bringing glory to God.

3. a. As a living sacrifice, holy and acceptable to God.
   b. (Your answer.) (Make choices that align with God's Word.)
   c. Reasonable service means for us to live our lives in a way that pleases Him because this is true worship. This is the right thing for us to do because God deserves it for the sacrifice He made for us through Jesus.

4. a. As unto the Lord; not unto men.

   b. b. No.

   c. (Your answer.)

5. a. The right way with wrong intentions; the wrong way; God's way.

   b. Choosing God's way will be the right thing to do; you will do it for the right reasons, and you will have the right attitude in the situation.

   c. Anchor your faith, enabling you to walk out God's Word daily.

   d. If it is coming out of a heart desiring to please God, not doing it out of obligation.

   e. To be devoted to God, you must want (desire) to do things that please Him, not do them just because He requires you to do them.

Key 5—Submit

1. To yield oneself to the authority or will of another; surrender.

2. a. Deny yourself and pick up your cross daily.

   b. You are not denying yourself of things; rather, you are choosing to humbly submit your will to God. You will do those things that please God.

   c. Every day.

3. We show our submission when we submit to government authority, church leadership, marriage, and in general to all Christians.

4. Strength.

5. a. In a self-determined act of obedience, Jesus prayed against His own desires (for the suffering that was to come to be removed from Him) but rather for God's will to be done.

   b. He's seated at God's right hand (a position of power) in heavenly places.

   c. He humbled Himself and became obedient to the point of death.

   d. God will exalt/promote us (to a place of honor in His service) at the appropriate time.

6. a. As we submit to God, we can boldly resist the devil, and he will flee from us.

   b. As we yield to God's authority and do things His way, we are able to use His authority on the earth. We are able to speak God's Word with power, pray for the sick and have them recover, cast out demons, and resist the devil as he flees. We have the power to put our flesh under subjection and allow Holy Spirit to do a new thing in us, for we are His workmanship created in Christ Jesus to do good works.

Key 6—Humble

1. A modest or low view of one's own importance.

2. a. Put others first; be considerate and allow someone else to have their way.

   b. Talk less / listen more; quickly admit to your mistakes; give compliments; serve others; be teachable; ask God for wisdom.

3. a. Someone who is wise, willing to learn, admits their limitations, listens very carefully, take notes, and applies what they've learned.

   b. (Your answer.)

   c. Pride and arrogance.

4. Pride ruins relationships. Those who are prideful have no need or room in their lives and hearts for God. They also don't admit wrong doing and even think they're better than the other person.

5. a. We receive grace, favor, promotion, honor, and wisdom. We are ultimately pleasing God because we are imitating Jesus. He, too, humbled Himself to the will and purpose of God.

   b. Jesus preached the good news, proclaimed deliverance to the captives, fed the poor, healed the sick, gave hope to the hopeless, and died for our sins.

   c. Share the Gospel, serve through a ministry at church, visit a nursing home, volunteer at a homeless shelter, serve others in your work capacity, and serve those in your home.

Key 7—Ask Every Day

1. a. (Your answer.)

   b. (Your answer.)

   c. (Your answer.)

   d. (Your answer.)

   e. No.

   f. If what you ask for is only for your pleasure, then you will not receive an answer from God.

   g. You receive an answer to your prayer when it lines up with God's will. When you delight yourself in the Lord, enjoy serving Him, and want to please Him. At that point, you will be devoted to God's desires.

2. God looks at our hearts to see if we are in faith or if we have an ulterior motive. Our hearts must be pure because that is the only way to please Him.

3. You must begin to offer praise and thanksgiving for the answered prayer.

4. It's already done.

5. You must believe that you have received (taken hold of) it spiritually even before you physically see it.

Key 8—Meditation and Application

1. a. Meditation is to focus specifically on a topic, reflect, and study so that you'll be able to apply it to your life. As you meditate, you allow God to speak His wisdom to you, causing you to be stable.

    b. Meditating on God's Word gives us insight into what He wants for us and what He wants from us. It gives us guidance in our daily walk of faith to fulfill the plan He has for our lives.

2. a. Thoughts, words are seeds.

    b. Choose your words carefully.

    c. Words shape your destiny, whether good or bad. Speak what God says so that you can see His Word come alive in your life.

3. a. Satan will distort the Word to get you to disobey God.

    b. Jesus.

    a. We defeat his attempts with the Word of God.

4. a. Good things.

    b. What you have been meditating (focusing) on the most is what will come out of your mouth under pressure.

    c. Yes; it shows whether or not you are trusting God (believing His Word).

    d. Repent and begin spending more time in the Word (desiring God).

5. a. When you hear and do God's Word, you're able to stand against the trials and tribulations that come to destroy you. It's your obedience to His Word that protects you. He will give you strength, wisdom, peace, and more to help you endure and bring you into victory.

    b. You lose. If you are not living God's Word, then you are not in faith and trusting Him. Without Jesus at the center of your life, you are headed for destruction.

    c. You must do what it says to do, act how it says to act, say what it says to say, and live how it says for you to live.

    d. Your life.

6. a. *Imitate* means to follow and to model yourself after someone.

    b. We walk (live) in love every day; God's unconditional, agape love.

7. a. (Your answer.)

    b. (Your answer.)

Key 9—Walk by the Spirit

1. Spirit, soul, and body.

2. To back away from (abandon, reject) your new life in Christ.

3. a. Hold your peace; keep your joy; be thankful; expect great things.

b. *Hold your peace* cultivates self-control and allows you to rely on the Lord's help. *Keeping your joy* is a powerful force used to defeat discouragement. *Being thankful* turns our hearts toward God, quickly sets our minds toward gratitude instead of complaining, and gives us a posture of humility. *Expecting great things* shows our confidence in the goodness of God.

4. a. Sexual immorality, impurity, idolatry, hatred, discord, jealousy, fits of rage, and so on.

   b. Love, joy, peace, patience, kindness, goodness, faithfulness, gentleness, and self-control.

   c. As you are walking in the Spirit (love, joy, and peace), you are acting and doing things contrary to world, and it keeps the desires of the flesh from developing.

   d. You win because you are not dominated by your emotions or external factors.

Key 10—Be Persistent

1. Continuing firmly or obstinately in a course of action in spite of difficulty or opposition.

2. (Your answer.)

3. We must be persistent in our faith in order to receive the benefits of God's Word.

4. It is building your character; you'll begin handling situations God's way instead of the world's way.

5. Love, joyfulness, kindness, humility, obedience, loyalty, patience, self-control, sincerity, truthfulness, and so on.

6. Yes. A believer can walk in anger, arrogance, unforgiveness, discouragement, depression, jealousy, strife, envy, lie, and so on.

7. a. Humbly surrender your will to God in faith (elevate His Word above your desires).

   b. Not yielding to Satan—not doing, saying, or dwelling on what he wants you to do but doing things God's way. (Satan's plan is to defeat you.)

8. Mighty to the pulling down of strongholds.

Printed in the United States
by Baker & Taylor Publisher Services